KINGDOM SEEKERS

A Guide to Personal Development

GEOFFREY MACHARIA

LIFE AND SUCCESS PUBLISHING
www.abookinsideyou.com

Copyright © Geoffrey Macharia 2010

All rights reserved. No part of this publication may be produced, distributed, or transmitted in any form or by any means, including photocopying, recording, or other electronic or mechanical methods, without the prior written permision of the publisher, except in the case of brief quotations embodied in critical reviews and certain other noncommercial uses permitted by copyright law.

For permission requests, write to the publisher, addressed "Attention: Permissions Coordinator" at the email address below:

Life and Success Media

e-mail: info@abookinsideyou.com

www.abookinsideyou.com

Unless otherwise stated, all scripture quotations are taken from the Holy Bible, New Living Translation (NLT). Other versions cited are NIV, NKJV, AMP and KJV. Quotations marked NIV are taken from the HOLY BIBLE, NEW INTERNATIONAL VERSION. Copyright © 1973, 1978, 1984 by International Bible Society. Used by permission of Hodder and Stoughton Ltd, a member of the Hodder Headline Plc Group. All rights reserved. "NIV" is a registered trademark of International Bible Society. UK trademark number 1448790.

Quotations marked KJV are from the Holy Bible, King James Version.

ISBN: 978-1-907402-98-2

Cover design: Allan Sealy

Contents

Biography 5

Dedication 7

Acknowledgement 9

Introduction 11

Chapter 1
Kingdom of God 13

Chapter 2
Spiritual Development 21

Chapter 3
Emotional Development 33

Chapter 4
Physical Development 43

Chapter 5
Mental Development 61

Chapter 6
 Time & Time management 71

Chapter 7
 Purpose 81

Chapter 8
 Conclusion 89

Biography

Rev Geoffrey is the senior Pastor of Rhema Covenant Ministries as well as a Politician in the United Kingdom. In 2004 he was elected as a member of LSP Local Strategic Partnership and later contested for the Greater London Assembly in the year 2008 and Parliamentary seat for Lambeth in 2010 general elections respectively. He holds a Bachelor of Commerce and a Diploma in Health and social sciences .He has ministered to thousands of people and has fostered 15 children by the time this book was written not to mention many Orphans he has helped in Africa. He is married to Charity and has two daughters Grace and Theresa.

Dedication

This book is dedicated to the true believers who worship God in truth and in spirit, and are struggling to apply the Kingdom principles in day to day's life. For we are encouraged to live lives worthy of God, who calls us into his kingdom and glorious blessedness into which true believers will enter after Christ's return.

To the young believers who are confused by wrong teachings and wrong doctrines emerging in our century.

And to the people of Rhema Covenant Ministries, your love, loyalty, support, dedication and enthusiasm are above all. I am committed to you, to help you to live your best live now and to be effective in the Kingdom. The future is even brighter.

Acknowledgement

Nothing in life is ever successful without the corporate effort of many gifted people who are willing to network and submit their talent, experience, and passion for a common goal. It takes a great team to make all the elements come together in any project including writing a book. This work is a product of countless individuals whose thoughts, ideas, perspectives, and work have given me the exposure to the knowledge I have placed in this book.I want to extend my personal and sincere thanks to:

Charity Macharia: my beautiful wife and our children **Grace** and **Theresa**, for their patience and understanding during my endless work and late nights writing. My achievements are yours also.

Dr Musa Ndengu: the great facilitator; without your expertise, this project wouldn't have been possible.

Thanks for encouraging me to put my teachings together in this book.

My Foster children: Beatty, Noble; Tegsti, Tesfy; cherish; Lika, Pilgrim, Tanya, Karina and Salam. You have taught me to be a servant in the community.

Ministers and members of Rhema Covenant Ministries. I have been blessed to work alongside you; you are the greatest church I have ever known

Introduction

I decided to write this book because I found out that many honest believers are struggling with their day to day lives. I also found out that many Kingdom seekers are seeking answers in the wrong directions. As a result they fall into the hands of false doctrines and exploitation. Proverbs 19: 2 desire without knowledge is not good.

This book is a step by step guide of a believers Journey, how to prepare a kingdom seeker, to be strong and be effective in his life.

It is true that God sent his son Jesus Christ to bring people into the Kingdom. **But to as many as did receive and welcome him. He gave the authority (power, privilege, right) to become the children of God. That is to those who believe in (adhere to, trust and rely on) his name. John 1:12**

What will a kingdom seeker do while waiting the everlasting kingdom? You face the same challenges like you had before you became a believer. While on earth, the body of the believer have the basic needs: food; clothing and shelter just like a none-believer. What did Jesus mean when he said that the Kingdom of God is here? Mark 1:15 Are we expecting another Kingdom or are we already living in the Kingdom.

These are some of the questions that this book will tempt to answer and many other questions to help you reader be more equipped for the good works which were assigned and prepared even before you were born.

For those whom he foreknew, he also destined from the beginning to be molded into the image of his Son Romans 8:29.

Chapter

The Kingdom of God

Jesus Christ preached the message of the Kingdom more than any other message demonstrating the power of his kingdom and the principles of this Kingdom.

> **He said to them (Disciples), I must preach the good news (The Gospel) of the Kingdom of God to the other cities also, for I was sent for this purpose.**
> **Luke 4:43**

When Jesus came to this world, God had already planned in advance what he was to do. He was a man of purpose. He was a man on mission. My fellow Kingdom seeker, when you were born, it was not by mistake, it does not matter where you were born, God does not make mistakes. You are a man or a woman on mission here on earth.

God created you for a purpose. For your purpose you were born.

Jesus Christ stated very clearly that his purpose was to introduce the Kingdom of God to the world. This is the good news; the gospel. He started by recruiting the twelve disciples who would carry on with the work of preaching the good news after his departure.

Kingdom Seeker, you are on a pilgrimage here on earth. We come for a short time for a purpose, and then we pass the mantle to the next generation who carry on with the work, for we are a big chain in the plans of God which were predestined before heavens and earth were created by the almighty God.

Our responsibility is to find our purpose, our calling, build our calling through preparation and practicing it until we perfect the calling and use it for the glory of the almighty God.

> **For we are God's (own) handiwork recreated that we may do those good works which God predestined (planned beforehand) for us, that we should walk in them. Ephesians 2:10.**

The Kingdom of God can be divided in three parts.

1. Where God lives in heaven.

   Isaiah 14:13 you (Satan) said in your heart I will ascend to heaven; I will exalt my throne above the

> stars of God; I will sit upon the mount of assembly in the uttermost north. I will ascend above the heights of the clouds; I will make myself like the most High.

Satan recognises the throne of the Almighty God in Heaven, he wanted that throne, but he was defeated and thrown out of Heaven. The throne is the domain of a King. A King has a domain called Kingdom. So the Almighty God is the king and his domain is Heaven. God lives in Heaven and rules from there. He is surrounded by angels.

2. The Kingdom of God on Earth

Genesis 1:26. God said, let us make mankind in our image, after our likeness, and let them have dominion over all creation on earth.

God created another kingdom which he placed man as the ruler. Man was to be the King here on earth and rule as it is in heaven. He created man in his own image. Man was created with the spirit of God; intellect and emotions. God was to rule the earth through man but there was a problem, Lucifer, a rebellious, fallen arch angel, known as Satan was thrown out of heaven, because he wanted to become a King, and out of malice, anger and deception, he came and took the right of man to rule the earth.

Now the serpent was more subtle and crafty than any living creature of the field which the lord God had made. And he (Satan) said to the woman, can it really be that God has said, you shall not eat from every tree of the garden. Genesis 3:1

3. The spiritual Kingdom on Earth

> And this good news of the kingdom will be preached throughout the whole world as a testimony to all the nations, and then will come to an end Mathew 24:14.

This was an answer to a question which the disciples had asked Jesus Christ concerning when the kingdom of God shall rule the world. As Israelites there was an expectation of a messiah who was to save Israel from their enemies. They expected Jesus Christ to overthrow the Roman Empire. But Jesus came to introduce the principles of the Kingdom of God which are righteousness and forgiveness from penalty of sin as a condition of entering the Kingdom of God. This will prepare the coming of Jesus Christ as the King in his second coming.

> Jesus answered, I assure you, most solemnly I tell you, that unless a person is born again, he cannot ever see the kingdom of God. John 3:3.

The Kingdom of God is coming, where Jesus Christ will rule the world as the King and the Kingdom seeker will rule with him. The Kingdom of earth will be returned to man as it was before Satan took over. This is going to happen when Jesus Christ comes back.

At the moment, the work of the Kingdom seeker is to preach the good news (the gospel) and to practice the principles of the Kingdom, while waiting the coming of Jesus Christ the King of Kings and Lord of Lords.

> Go then and make disciples of all the nations, baptizing them into the name of the father and of the son and of the Holy Spirit. Teach them to observe everything that I have commanded you. And behold, I am with you all the days to the end. Mathew 28 19-:20

When Jesus Christ said that the Kingdom of God is at hand, what did he mean?

The bible is very clear of how the Kingdom of God here on earth will be like.

> Behold a King will reign in righteousness, and princes will rule with Justice. And each one of them shall be like a hiding place from the wind and a shelter from the storm, like streams of water in a dry place, like the shade of a great rock in a weary land. Then the eyes of those who see will not be closed or dimmed, and the ears of those who hear will listen. And the mind of the rash

> will understand knowledge and have a good judgement, and the tongue of the stammered will speak readily and plainly. Isaiah 32:1-4.

The kingdom of God will be ruled with justice and righteousness. There will be no pains or trouble, famine and wars will not be experienced; poverty and sicknesses will not be in the Kingdom of God.

> God will wipe away every tear from their eyes; and death shall be no more, neither shall there be anguish nor grief nor pain any more, for the old conditions and the former order of things have passed away. Revelation 21: 4

It is very clear that we are not yet in the Kingdom of God; why, the whole world is in pain, the recession, the famine, wars; diseases; pestilences; volcanic ash and death are affecting the rich; the poor, the mighty.

> We know that the whole creation has been morning together in the pains of labour until now, and not only the creation, but we ourselves too, who have and enjoy the first fruits of the Holy Spirit groan inwardly as we wait for the redemption of our bodies. Romans 8:22-23.

The whole creations including those who are born again are groaning, if the Believers are in the Kingdom as yet, they could not be experiencing pain. The last enemy to be defeated will be death. Today even believers are experiencing death. As believers we have hope in the coming of Jesus Christ, his salvation and the new heavens and earth.

> **The prayer Jesus taught his disciples was: Our father who is at in heaven, hallowed be your name, your kingdom come, your will be done on earth as it is in heaven. Mathew 6:9-10.**

You do not pray for what you already have, you give thanks for what you have for example; you give thanks for food before you eat. You pray for the Kingdom to come because it is not yet here (in full) on earth.

Golden Truths:

You are on earth for a purpose
It is your responsibility to discover your purpose
God does not make mistakes
The Kingdom of God is coming
You cannot enter the Kingdom of God unless you are born again

Chapter

Spiritual Development

Before we can be of use in the Kingdom of God, there is a time for preparation, the time to develop and a time for training. In the gospel of Luke 2:52 the scripture says that Jesus grew both in body and in wisdom, gaining favour with God and men. Even Jesus took time to grow and develop before he could become the saviour of the world. He developed physically and he developed in wisdom.

If a Kingdom seeker will be effective in the world, he needs to develop .If you fail to plan, you plan to fail. Success is a total sum of knowledge; character and environment S=K+C+E.

A seeker of the kingdom will need to develop spiritually, mentally; physically and emotionally. Jesus is preparing his church to reign with him, for we are joint heirs with him, but it will be a disaster if he comes for the church which is not ready to rule with him. It is the responsibility of every individual believer and the church to train themselves in all the four areas.

We shall now look into all the four areas and compare with what the scriptures say about them.

Four steps of Spiritual Development

Step 1. Read the Bible Daily

Man lives by every word that proceeds out of God's mouth Deuteronomy 8:3

Faith comes by hearing, and by hearing the word of God: Romans 10:17

Every Scripture is God breathed and profitable for instruction, for reproof and conviction of sin, for correction of error and discipline and obedience, for training in righteousness.2 Timothy 3:16

Your word is a lamp to my feet and a light to my path psalms 119: 105.

For the commandment is a lamp, and the whole teaching of the law is light, and reproofs of discipline are the way of life. Proverbs 6:23.

The word implanted and rooted in your hearts, contains the power to save your souls James 1:21.

It is obvious from the scriptures above that the more you read the word daily the more you develop faith; the more you understand what is right and what is wrong; the more you become wise. Your spirit needs to be fed daily just like your body needs food daily.

The Holy Spirit will use the seeker more who knows the word. The Holy Spirit communicates to the seeker through the words confirmed by the Scriptures since he is the author of the word.

The effectiveness of the seeker's prayer is in proportion to the seeker's knowledge of the scripture.

God honours his word in fact he has exalted his word above his name. Psalms 138:2. This means that whatever God says, he will do. For his words are never void. What God has promised is yes and amen. As a believer then, you need to know the word of God so that you can remind God of his promises.

> For as the rain and snow come down from heavens, and return not there again, but water the earth and make it bring forth and sprout, that it may give seed to the sower and bread to the eater, so shall my word be that goes out of my mouth; it shall not return to me void, but it shall accomplish that

> which I please and purpose, and it shall prosper in the thing for which I sent it. Isaiah 55:10-11.

The more we read the word, the more you understand God and the more he speaks to you. So Read your Bible every day.

God spoke to Joshua the successor of Moses, that if he wanted to succeed, as a leader, he had to study and meditate day and night the bible.

Joshua 1:8 Do not let this book of the law depart from your mouth; meditate on it day and night, so that you may be careful to do everything written in it. Then you will be prosperous and successful.

David a very successful King said: blessed is the man who delights in the law of the Lord and on his law he meditates day and night. Whatever he does prospers. Psalms 1:2

Step2. Become a church member

You need a mentor. Choose a pastor who will help you grow in the word. You need to surround yourself with believers in a church. While choosing a Church, pray about it, then investigate whether the Church you want to join, is a full gospel church, is it a bible led church. You need to be careful for not all churches are serving

God. You need to investigate about the leadership of the Church. Are the leaders Godly people, their integrity; honesty and reputation in the surrounding community, are they respected. 1Timothy 3 gives guidance of the Bishops and Deacons in the church, how they should conduct themselves. So before joining a church make sure that the leadership conform to the instructions given to Timothy and Titus by Paul on how to select church Leadership. Mostly it is to deal with the character of elders in the church and the doctrine. Once you have established a Church, join and become a member by submitting yourself to the church authority. In the Kingdom of God, there are no lone rangers, the church functions as a body. 1Corinthians 12 is written to show us how the body of Christ works. Although members have different gifts, they all come from the Holy Spirit. We are baptised in the name of Jesus but have different functions in the body. The body of Christ works as a team. It is in the church that you learn how to serve God. How can you love the God you have never seen if you cannot love your neighbour?

It is in the church you learn how to submit and to serve, you learn in the church how to work in the Kingdom of God. In the world the boss loads other people, in the kingdom the greatest becomes a servant.

In the world it is always about self. In the Kingdom it is about others.

In the world it is success. In the Kingdom it is about giving God glory.

step 3. get involved in a ministry

It is in the Ministry that you identify your gift. The Holy Spirit distributes different gifts to different believers due to the power of divine grace operating in their souls but he remains the same. The gifts are the special endowments of supernatural energy.

There are various gifts in the body of Christ. The gift of preaching, teaching, word of wisdom; healing; miracles; faith; speaking in tongues; governance; Helps and many other types of gifts.1 Corinthians 12:8-10. It is in the ministry you learn your gift. For example, most of the celebrated secular music artists today trace their roots in the church. Others started helping and ended up with world known organisations like world vision; Red Cross; feed the children' All these people started from humble beginnings in the Churches Ministry. Ministry comes from the word serve. A minister is a servant. Many believers remain babies in the church since they do not want to participate in the church and hence they will never discover what God called them to become. Once they remain babies, then there are chances of being abused and exploited by false prophets. God does not call spectators but participants. You are a co-worker with God; a joint heir with Jesus Christ

> **External religious worship that is pure and unblemished in the sight of God the father is this: to visit and help and care for the orphans and widows in their affliction and need and to keep oneself unspotted and uncontaminated from the world. James 1:27**
>
> **For as the human body apart from the spirit is lifeless, so faith apart from its works of obedience is also dead.James2:26.**
>
> **We will continue to devote ourselves steadfastly to prayer and the ministry of the word Acts 6:4.**

God has given you a gift, that gift will make room for you. You will not serve ordinary people, you will serve among Kings. This begins as humble beginnings in the ministry. Get involved in a ministry and release your gift in the Hands of God and he well exalt you in due time.

step 4. pray every day

Prayer is simply communicating with God.

Communication is important in every relationship. Many marriages are breaking because of lack of communication; nations are going to wars because of misunderstanding each other. Brothers are fighting each other and cannot see eye to eye. Why? It is Because of Lack of communication or poor communication.

Communication gives information; instructions; warning; advice; encouragement; understanding and expresses the feelings of a person.

In Genesis 3:9 the lord God called to Adam and said to him, where are you? God created man so that he could have fellowship with him. He used to talk to Adam, there used to be communication; it was until Satan made both Adam and Eve sin against God that the Communication ended. I thank God for the second Adam (Jesus Christ) who restored back the communication.

When Jesus Christ said it is finished and died at the cross, the curtain at the temple which divided Holy of Holies from the rest of the Temple tore from the top to bottom, meaning that God had opened communication once again and every person had access to the mercy seat and could talk to God through Jesus Christ. Hebrews 10: 19-20.

God wants to talk to you. You are precious before God. Life can put you down; challenges of life can oppress, suppress and depress you. You may be feeling low; unwanted; people may reject you, but God will never reject you, whoever calls upon the name of the lord will be saved. Jesus is calling you. He is saying, come unto me all you who are heavily laden and I will give you rest. Cast your burden unto him for he cares for you. He wants to help; he wants to be your friend, your brother and your saviour. Won't you let him? Talk to him, call unto him, for this reason he came to this world so that those who would believe in him will have eternal life.

Examples:

Elijah the prophet was a man with feelings just like us. He feared a woman called Jezebel; he was thirsty; hungry; angry and tired but he prayed earnestly to God and God answered his prayers.

> **Elijah was a human being with a nature such as we have (with feelings; affections, and constitution like ours) and he prayed earnestly for it not to rain, and no rain fell on the earth for three years and six months, and then he prayed again and the Heavens supplied rain and the land produced its crops as usual James 5: 17-18.**

King Solomon was a young man when he took over the mantle of leadership from his father. He prayed for wisdom to rule God's people and God granted his request. King Solomon a man full of wisdom, build God a temple, He made sacrifice and then prayed to God. God answered his prayers and promised that if his people prayed or petitioned him he would answer and heal their land.

> If my people, who are called by my name, shall humble themselves, pray, seek, crave, and require of necessity my face and turn from their wicked ways, then will I hear from heaven, forgive their sin, and heal their land. Now my eyes will be open and my ears attentive to prayer offered in this place 2 Chronicles 7:14-15

Moses was called by God and was promised by God that he will deliver God's people from Egypt and will worship God at Mount Sinai. True to his words Moses delivered Israelite from Egypt and came to worship God at Mount Sinai. God spoke to Moses and called him to the top of Mount Sinai to give him instructions.

> The lord came down upon Mount Sinai to the top of the mountain, and the lord called Moses to the top of the Mountain, and Moses went up. Exodus 19: 20.

Jesus Christ was a man of prayers; he was always in constant communication with his Heavenly father in Heaven. He could not do anything without asking the father. Towards the end of his ministry he prayed for his Disciples and those who would believe the message of his disciples, that they may be one; that they be protected from the evil.

> I am praying for them. I am not praying for the world, but for those you have given me, for they belong to you. John 17:9.

Jesus is a perfect example for us to imitate. If the Son of God prayed for everything while on earth what about us. Every Great man and woman in the Bible was a person of prayer. Those who stopped praying, they became victims of Satan. Jesus; Moses; David; Esther; Deborah; Hannah; Daniel; Abraham; Paul; Cornelius; Philip; Steven, they were all prayerful Men.

When King Solomon stopped praying and turned his heart to other Gods, he fell from grace.

Today the pioneers of faith in our century are men of prayers. Late Kenneth Huggins; D.L.Moody; H.Spurgeon Dr T.L.Osborne; Billy Graham; Oral Roberts; Late D.G.S. Dhinakharan; Pastor Mathew Ashimolowo; Pastor Ambessa and Dr Hugh Osgood to mention but a few are all men of prayers. Political figures who have left a mark in this world were people of prayers. Abraham Lincoln, Ronald Reagan, and William Wilberforce to mention but a few. The list is indefinite.

Prayers move mountains
Prayers give us peace
Prayers acknowledges God as supreme

Prayers invite God to take charge in our lives. And if God is for us who can be against us?

Golden Truths

To grow spiritually you need

Step 1. Read the Bible every Day

Step2. Pray every day

Step3. Join a True Bible led Church

Step 4.Be active get involved in a ministry group

Chapter 3

Emotional Development

> For this very reason, make every effort to add to your faith goodness; and to goodness, knowledge; and to knowledge, self-control; and to self-control, perseverance; and to perseverance, godliness; and to godliness, brotherly kindness; and to brotherly kindness, love. For if you possess these qualities, in increasing measure, they will keep you from being ineffective and unproductive in your knowledge of our lord Jesus Christ. 2 Peter 1:5-8.

The purpose of emotional development is two way: first is to protect the Seeker and second is to make the seeker become effective and productive in His calling and in the knowledge of Jesus Christ.

> **Make every effort to live in peace with all men and to be holy; without holiness no one will see the lord. See to it that no one misses the grace of God and that no bitter root grows up to cause trouble and defile many. Hebrews 12: 14-15**

Bitterness is an emotion, if allowed to grow in a person, it causes trouble to the person who becomes negative, he or she losses hope and defile many people who come into contact with the bitter person

Definition: Oxford Dictionary:

Emotion means: intense mental feeling.

Emotions are our feelings.

Our emotions cause us to want and not to want, and when we have what we wanted, we then have emotions about owning it.

There are different types of emotions:

Emotions of wanting: Hope, love; anticipation; faith; desire; interest; courage; sometimes they lead to greed and envy

Emotions of not wanting: Fear; shame; anxiety; contentment; disgust; hate

Emotions of Having: happiness; Joy; pride; guilt and Jealousy;

Emotions of not having: Anger; sadness; distress; grief; despair.

PURPOSE OF EMOTIONS

1. **Motivation.** Emotions act to motivate us. Motivations are felt in the body. Our muscles tense or relax. Our emotions can make us feel uncomfortable or comfortable.

2. **Internal Signal.** When we think about something that contradicts our values, our emotions will tell us that this is bad. When we think about something that could hurt us, our emotions will tell us that this is not a good idea. Just by imagining what might happen, our emotions are still triggered and hence let us make better decisions.

3. **Social Signals.** We generally wear our hearts on our sleeves, as our inner emotions are displayed in our outer bodies. Our faces, in particular have around 90 muscles 30 of which have the sole purpose of signalling emotion to other people. Signals are generally very useful; as they help others decide how to behave towards

us. If someone is looking Angry, then attacking them is probably not a good idea. If they are looking afraid then you could attack them or you could help them thus earn their gratitude.

You can use emotions to motivate people. You connect good emotions with what you want them to do and bad emotions with what is not wanted. You can respond to the signals you see in other people. You can tell when somebody wants to be left alone; when they need to be comforted.

If you watch your own emotions, they are signals that tell you something about what is happening in the inner you. This can be very useful as we often do not realize what is going on in that deep, dark subconscious inside of us.

Positive and Negative Emotions

There are more negative emotions than positive emotions. We can feel; fear; anger; shame; hate and yet beyond basic happiness and joy there are a few positive feelings. A reason for this is because most emotions are designed to keep us alive. They signal warnings and prompt us to act, from running away to avoiding others to fighting back.

RESPONSIBILTY:

Emotional intelligence means taking primary responsibility for your own emotions and happiness. It is our duty to take primary responsibility for our own emotions and happiness. You cannot say that others made you feel the way you feel. Although they may be instrumental, the responsibility is yours, just as if you kill someone, there is no argument that says that someone else made you do it. In the Scriptures, Cain was told by God that he could master his emotions otherwise sin was encroaching on his heart.

> Then the Lord said to Cain "why are you angry? Why is your face downcast? If you do what is right, will you not be accepted? But if you do not do what is right, sin is crouching at your door, it desires to have you, but you must master it. Genesis 4:6-7.

BALANCING

The ability to balance emotions and reason in making decisions leads to good Decisions. Emotion should not be abandoned, lest cold and callous decisions are made. Nor should logic be abandoned unless you want a wishy-washy outcome.

Emotions are one of the main things that derail communications and rationalism goes out of the window. If you can identify and control your own emotions, you have a better chance of winning any argument, if you can sense the emotions of others; you have a chance to change them. And of course it all starts with yourself and your own emotions.

Emotion Arousal Triggers.

In the Song of Solomon 2:7 the writer identifies emotional arousal and said: **I charge you do not arouse or awaken love until it so desire"**

Arousal often happens through a Trigger, which appears through our senses. Thus for example arousal can happen through.

Touch: could be a punch, kiss or caress

Vision: Seeing something shocking or desirable

Hearing: A sudden noise or somebody saying something

Smell: An evocative odour that triggers powerful memories

Taste: could of wonderful or disgusting food

By understanding the process by which people become aroused, you can gain control of whether and how arousal happens. The first place to start with this is yourself. If you become emotionally aroused, then you are losing some control. This is not a good thing, so learning self-control can be a critical skill.

In the second letter of Peter Chapter1:5; the Apostle advices the kingdom seeker to add Self-control to knowledge.

Prophet Hosea speaking on behalf of God said; my people are destroyed from lack of Knowledge. Hosea 4:6

In the book of John 10:10 Jesus said that the thief comes only to steal and kill and destroy. The thief is Satan and he uses our emotions to accomplish his mission of stealing what belongs to us, he kills our joy, our happiness and finally our souls, he destroys us through our ignorance or lack of knowledge.

Satan used the emotions of Eve to still from mankind their created right and promise of having dominion on earth. He tempted Jesus for forty days in the desert using the same formula of appealing to Jesus emotions. He tempted Lust of eyes; then used lust of flesh, and finally pride of life. Jesus defeated Satan because he (Jesus) had a proper knowledge of the scriptures. Luke 4:1-13

Kingdom seeker, If Satan did not spare Jesus Christ, he will not spare you either. You better know how to handle your emotions. In the letter of James 1:13, James's advice is that when tempted, no one should say God is tempting me, for God cannot be tempted by evil, nor does he tempt anyone, but each one is tempted when, by his own evil desire, he is dragged away and enticed. Then after desire has conceived, it gives birth to sin, and sin when it is full grown gives birth to death.

Like God told Cain, as a Child of God, The most high wants you to develop and master your emotions.

SEVEN DEADLY SINS

All the seven deadly sins and all the seven virtues are emotions.

Pride: Excessive belief in one's own ability

Envy: Wanting what others have. Be it status, ability or possessions

Gluttony: Desire to eat or consume more than you require

Lust: A powerful craving for such as sex, power and money

Anger: Is the loss of rational self-control and the desire to harm others.

Greed: Is the desire for material wealth or gain

Sloth: Is Laziness and the avoidance of work

THE SEVEN CARDINAL VIRTUES:

The seven virtues are:

Faith: Is belief in the right things (Including Virtues)

Hope: Is taking a positive future view that good will prevail.

Charity: Is concern for and active helping of others.
Fortitude: or courage is never giving up
Justice: Is being fair and equitable with others
Prudence: Is care of and moderation with money
Temperance: Is moderation of needed things and abstinence from things which are not needed.

SELF-AWARENESS

By being emotionally self-aware means: knowing how you are feeling in a given time. Self- knowledge is the first step in being able to handle emotions. If you can see them and name them, then at least you have a chance to do something about them.

Golden Truths

Emotions are our feelings
You are responsible of your own emotions
When we feel something, we consequently respond to the feeling
The purpose of emotions is motivation; internal signals and social signals
Emotions are aroused by our common senses, touch; vision; hearing; smell and taste.
When you understand the process of emotion arousal you gain self-control.

Chapter

Physical Development

Physical development is simply development of the body.

The aim of this chapter is to help the seeker maintain physical fitness to be able to do the work of God. If Jesus Christ was not healthy, it was very difficult to carry the cross to Golgotha having gone through all the torture he went through. Luke 2: 52 And Jesus grew in wisdom and Stature (body) and in favour with God and Man. Time does not allow me to go into details about Moses, David; Joshua; Daniel; Caleb ;Samson and many Heroes in the Bible who did exploits for the Lord. The book of Hebrews chapter 11 mentions these Heroes and their exploits. They needed their bodies to carry out their calling. You have a calling; God has called you at a time like this for a purpose. You need a body and a healthy body to fulfil your calling.

Your body is the Temple of the Holy Spirit; you carry the Spirit of God wherever you go, just like the priests of the Old Testament used to carry the Ark of God. Although we live in the jars of clay, we have the hidden treasure, which is the Spirit of God in our bodies. **I Corinthians 6:18 Do you not know that your body is a Temple of the Holy Spirit, who is in you, whom you have received from God? You are not your own. You were bought at a price. Therefore honour God with your body.**

It then goes without saying that since our bodies are the Temples of the Holy Spirit; we need to take care of them. For our bodies to be fit and healthy, we need three vital elements: Exercise, nutrition and rest.

A: EXERCISE:

Apostle Paul instructs his protégé Timothy in 1Timothy 4:8 that physical training is of some value, but spiritual training is useful and of value in everything and in every way. Apostle Paul puts value in physical training.

There are four stages of Physical development

1. Childhood physical development
2. Adolescence physical development

3. Adulthood physical development
4. Old age physical development

CHILDHOOD PHYSICAL DEVELOPMENT

A child's physical development depends on Nature and nurture. On one hand a child is born with genetic map that will guide such matters as height and general muscle development. The parent can do nothing about Nature. But on the other side the child's environment will influence the overall health and activity levels which contribute to physical development; it is expected that the carer or parent of the child will encourage the child's development through proper nutrition and appropriate physical activity.

In order for children to further their physical development, they must practice the many skills that will lead to gross balance and coordination of their bodies. Children should be encouraged to engage in activities that will offer the chance to walk, run, jump and throw.

ADOLESCENCE PHYSICAL DEVELOPMENT

The development of children ages 12 years through 18 years old is expected to include predictable physical and mental milestones.

Adolescence is characterized by dramatic physical changes moving the individual from childhood into physical maturity. Early adolescence changes are noted with the appearance of secondary sexual characteristics. Girls may begin to develop breast as early as 8 years old, with full breast development achieved anywhere between 12 to 18 years. Pubic hair growth as well as armpit and leg hair begins at about age 9 or 10 and reaches adult distribution patterns at about 13 to 14 years. Menstrual periods (Menarche) occur between 10 years and 15 years. A rapid growth in height occurs for girls between the ages of about 10 and 15 years peaking somewhere around 12 years. A rapid growth in height occurs for boys between the ages of about 10 to 12 and 16 to 18, peaking around 14. During this time voice change in boys occurs as the body changes.

BEHAVOIUR

The sudden rapid physical changes that adolescents experience typically lend this period of development to be one of self- consciousness, sensitivity and concern over one's own body changes, and excruciating comparisons between oneself and one's peers. Since physical changes may not occur in a smooth, regular schedule, adolescents may go through stages of awkwardness, both in terms of appearance and physical mobility and coordination, unnecessary anxieties may arise if adolescent girls are not informed and prepared for the onset of menstrual periods or if adolescent boys are not provided accurate information about nocturnal emissions (wet dreams) which occur at this stage.

During adolescence, it is appropriate for youngsters to begin to separate from their parents and establish an individual identity, in some cases, this may occur with minimal reaction on the part of all involved. In some families however, significant conflict may arise over adolescents acts of rebellion, and the parents needs to maintain control and have the youth comply. As adolescents pull away from parents in search of identity, the peer group takes on a special significance. It may become a safe haven, in which adolescent can test new ideas and compare physical and psychological growth. In early adolescence, the peer group usually consists of non-romantic friendships, often including gangs or clubs. Members of the peer group often attempt to behave alike; dress alike; have secret codes or rituals, and participate in the same activities. As the youth moves into mid-adolescence that is 14 to 16 years and beyond the peer group expands to include romantic friendships. Mid- to- late adolescence is characterized by a need to establish sexual identity through becoming comfortable with one's own body and sexual feelings. Through romantic friendships, dating, and experimentation, adolescents learn to express and receive intimate or sexual advances in a comfortable manner that is consistent with internalized values. **Young people who do not have the opportunity for such experiences may demonstrate difficulty in establishing intimate relationships into adulthood.**

Behaviour Demonstrated

1. **Self-centredness.** The adolescents spend so much time thinking about and looking at themselves, they become conscious thinking everybody is thinking about them. They do not realize that their peers are also thinking about themselves.

2. **Indestructible Self.** This belief feeds the Notion that something bad will never happen to me, only the other person. In this sense something bad may represent becoming pregnant or catching sexually transmitted disease having un-protected intercourse; causing a car crash while driving under the influence of drugs or alcohol or over speeding; developing oral cancer as a result of chewing tobacco, or any of the many adverse effects of a wide range of risk-taking behaviours.

SAFETY:

Adolescent safety issues stem from increased strength and agility that may develop before they have developed good decision making skills; a strong need for peer approval, coupled with the myths of adolescence, may entice a young person to attempt hazardous adventures or participate in a variety of risk- taking behaviours. Appropriate motor vehicle safety should be emphasized, focusing on the role of driver, passenger and pedestrian, the influence of substance abuse, and the importance of seat belts. Young people need to be aware of the potential dangers including sudden death which may occur not only with regular substance abuse, but even experimental use of drugs and alcohol. If adolescents appear to be isolated from peers, un-interested in school or social activities, or deteriorating in performance at school, work or sports, psychological evaluation may be necessary. Many adolescents are at increased risk of depression and potential suicide attempts, due to pressures and conflicts that may arise within families, Schools or social organisations, and intimate relationships.

Parenting tips for adolescents.

1. Adolescents usually require privacy in which to contemplate the changes taking place in their bodies. Ideally the youth should be allowed to

have a private bedroom.

2. Teasing an adolescent child about physical changes is inappropriate, because it may cause self- consciousness and embarrassment.

3. Parents need to remember that the adolescent's interest in body changes and sexual topics is natural, normal development and does not necessarily indicate movement into sexual activity.

4. Parents must take care not to label emerging drives and behaviours as wrong; immoral or demonic they need to guide and give proper information regarding the changes in the child.

5. A child's attraction to the parent of the opposite sex is common during adolescent years. Healthy parents deal with this by acknowledging the physical changes and attractiveness of the child without crossing appropriate parent-child relationship boundaries.

6. Parents should be prepared for and recognize that there are common conflicts that may develop while parenting adolescents.

7. Parents can anticipate their authority to be repeatedly challenged, as children enter more through their adolescent years.

Adulthood Physical Development:

Development takes a new meaning in adulthood because the process is no longer defined by physical and cognitive growth spurts. Adulthood, which encompasses the majority of a person's life span, is marked instead by considerable psychosocial gains that are coupled with steady but slow physical decline.

The young adult years usually between 17 and 40 are often referred to as the peak years. Young adults experience excellent health, vigour, and physical functioning. Young adults have not yet been subjected to age-related physical deterioration, such as wrinkles, weakened body systems, and reduced lung and heart capacities. Their strength, coordination, reaction time, sensation (sight; hearing; taste; smell and touch), fine motor skills, and sexual response are at a maximum.

Both men and women enjoy the benefit of society's emphasis on youthfulness .They typically look and feel attractive and sexually appealing. Young men may have healthy skin, all or most of their hair, and well defined muscles. Young women may have soft skin, a small waist line; toned legs, thighs and buttocks. With good looks, great health, and plenty of energy, young adults dream and set plans. Adults in their 20's and 30's set many goals that they intend to accomplish, from finishing universities to getting married and raising children, to becoming a millionaire before age 30. Young adulthood is a time when nothing seems impossible. With the right attitude and enough persistence and energy, anything can be achieved.

Middle Adulthood Physical development

The average life expectancy for adults is 75 years and 80 if you are strong Psalms 90:10.

The age of 50 is the middle adulthood though this generally ranges from 45to 64. Many people at this age are busy with their career; families and preparing for retirement. It's important that they are aware of the physical development occurring in middle adulthood.

Hearing and Vision

The ability to hear high pitched noises disappears progressively during middle adulthood as most people begin recognizing hearing loss around the age 40. Vision also decreases for both sexes, as their ability to focus declines, and they need brighter lights to see.

Strength and Coordination

As adults pass through middle adulthood their strength begins to diminish. Some of their muscles is replaced with fat. Flexibility also decreases, and the reaction time of individuals in middle adulthood decreases as well.

Sexuality

The start of middle adulthood often signifies the end of a woman's ability to bear children. They proceed to go through menopause during the middle age stage in their life. Men still possess the ability to reproduce although their fertility decreases in middle adulthood as they age.

Diseases

Diabetes, Heart diseases, and cancer are just a few of the common diseases discovered during middle adulthood, while chances are that these diseases have been building up in an individual throughout their life, the discovering and treatment of them occurs when people are in middle age.

PHYSICAL APPEARANCE

The changes in physical appearance are some of the most notable parts of many people as they experience middle adulthood physical development. Hair begins to turn gray or white; Teeth fade from white to yellow; more wrinkles appear, especially on the face and skin begins to sag.

Considerations:

While humans can't stop the aging process all together, there are some things that individuals in this life stage can do to slow the physical developments that are occurring. Regular exercise, stretching and strength training can help to minimize the loss of flexibility, coordination and strength.

Maintaining regular appointments and screening by your Doctor can alert you to potential health problems giving you the opportunity to seek treatment early and prevent further complications and problems.

OLD AGE PHYSICAL DEVELOPMENT

The late adulthood period are those years that encompass age 65 and beyond.

Gerontology is the study of old age or the study of old age and aging and how to confront Ageism including fighting discrimination due to old age. Aging inevitably mean's physical decline, some of which may be due to lifestyle, such as poor diet and luck of exercise, rather than illness or the aging process energy reserves dwindle.

Physical Changes

There is often a general physical decline, and people become less active, Old age can cause, amongst other things.

1. Wrinkles and liver spots on the skin
2. Change of hair colour to grey or white
3. Hair loss
4. Lessened hearing
5. Diminished eye sight
6. Slower reaction times and agility
7. Reduced ability to think clearly
8. Difficulty recalling memories
9. Lessening or cessation of sex
10. Greater susceptibility to bone diseases such as osteoarthritis.

Note: While the physical deteriorates, wisdom increases Job 12:12

NUTRITION

Nutrition is eating a healthy balanced diet. Nutrition is the second element and very essential for physical development. A good diet is central to overall good health, but you must know the best food to include in your meals and those best to avoid.

The key to a healthy balanced diet is not to ban or omit any foods or food groups but to balance what you eat by consuming a variety of foods from each food group in the right proportions for good health.

There are five food groups on the eat well plate:

Fruit and vegetables

Bananas; mangoes; Oranges; Pears etc

These should make up about a third of your daily diet and can be eaten as part of every meal, as well as being first choice for a snack. You should eat at least five portions of fruit and vegetables each day. Research suggests this can help to protect against cancer, obesity and various chronic diseases such as Heart diseases. This is because of the unique package of nutrients and plant compounds they contain.

Starch/Carbohydrates

Bread; rice; potatoes and Pasta

This food group should make about a third of your daily diet and contains the starchy carbohydrates that are the body's main source of energy. When selecting products from this food group, chose unrefined carbohydrates over those that have been refined, as the unrefined products contain whole of the g-rain. Whole grain foods are rich in fibre and other nutrients that have many health benefits, and people who consume whole grains seem to have a reduced risk of certain cancers, diabetes and coronary heart disease.

The Final third of the eat- well plate is made up of three groups containing foods that need to be consumed in small proportions than the other two principle categories. These food groups contain nutrients essential to our diet, so it is important not to leave them out altogether.

Milk and Dairy Products

These should be eaten in moderation because of their high saturated content, but they are important source of calcium, which is essential for healthy bones and teeth. Choose low-fat or reduced-fat version.

Meat; Fish; eggs and beans

Protein

This food group includes both animal and plant sources of protein which is major functional and structural component of all cells. Protein provides the body with between 10 to 15% of its dietary energy, and is needed for growth and repair.

Foods and Drinks High in Fat or Sugar

This group makes up the smallest section on the eat-well plate. And includes foods that should be eaten sparingly, because although they are important energy source, they contain few nutrients and are often known as" empty calories".

Foods from this group are high in unhealthy components such as saturated fat; sugar and salt all of which are associated with an increased risk of developing certain diseases. They should only be eaten as occasional treats, or to increase the palatability of other important foods (such as sprinkling of sugar on some fruits or cream on some salads)

How to eat a balanced Diet

Eat a variety of foods to obtain all of the essential Nutrients.

Too much as well as too little can be bad for you balance is required

Every one's plate will look slightly different as we all have different requirements depending on our body's shape and size, and our level of activities.

How to Maintain a Balanced Diet

Base meals on starchy food

Eat lots of fruits and vegetables

Eat more fish

Cut down on saturated fat and sugar

Try to eat less salt

Get active and try to be a healthy weight watcher

Drink plenty of water

Always seek medical advice from your Doctor. It is important to have medical check up at least once a year. Even your vehicle has MOT once a year. Your body is more important than your vehicle.

When your energy intake (food eaten) is more than energy output (exercise) the result will be overweight and finally obesity.

Obesity is caused by lack of exercise and overeating.

Having discussed about exercise and nutrition, the third element to physical development is Rest. The body needs rest to recapture the energy lost during exercise.

C: REST

We have to sleep because it is essential to maintain normal levels of cognitive skills such as speech, memory; innovative and flexibility thinking, in other words, sleep plays a significant role in brain development.

If you do not sleep, the serious effects on our brains ability to function will be understated. After just one night without sleep, concentration becomes more difficulty and attention span shortens considerably.

Sleep deprived individuals have difficulty in responding to rapidly changing situations and making rational judgements. When you drive on motor ways in UK and many other countries you see signs warning that tiredness kills or driving while tired can cause accident so take a break. Always remember to take a brake. A change is as good as a rest.

Even God had to rest after six days work in the book of Genesis 2: 2-3

Golden truths

For physical development you need:
1. Exercise
2. Nutrition
3. Rest

Chapter 5

Mental Development

All human beings possess one thing which is far more valuable than any other possession. That one thing is our mind. When we recognize the value of our mind, we are able to guard it this is an aspect of mental development. In the book of proverbs 4:23 the word says that guard your mind because all the issues of life spring from our minds.

Cognitive development is the construction of thought process, including remembering, problem solving, and decision-making from childhood through adolescence to adulthood.

Cognitive development refers to how a person perceives, thinks, and gains understanding of his or her world through interaction of genetic and learned factors. Among the areas of cognitive development are information processing, intelligence, reasoning, language development and memory.

The mind is the battle field. If you have victory in the mind then you have more chances to have victory in life. The word says as far as you can see or perceive with your mind then you have it. Our thoughts determine what we say, what we say points our action. Our action forms our character and our character determines our destiny.

Mental development helps our mental capacity to perceive things and make proper decisions in life. The bible encourages us to pursue Knowledge; wisdom and understanding. Capacity building involves knowledge (Skills), wisdom and understanding.

KNOWLEDGE

Proverbs 19:2 Desire without knowledge is not good, and to be overhasty is to sin and miss the mark. Desire is an emotion (refer to emotion development) but knowledge is acquired through learning, information and association. **Proverbs 18:15 the mind of the prudent is ever getting knowledge and the ear of the wise is ever seeking knowledge.**

Definition:

1. General : Human faculty resulting from interpreted information; understanding that germinates from combination of data information, experience, and individual interpretation, variously defined as things that are held to be true in a given context and that drive us to action if there were no impediments.

   Capacity to act; justified true belief that increases an entity's capacity for effective action.

   Knowledge is the sum of what is known and resides in the intelligence and the competence of people.

   In Economics, Knowledge is recognized as a factor of production in its own right and distinct from labour known as Knowledge capital.

Law: Awareness or understanding of circumstances or fact, gained through association or experience.

Knowledge is power and when you use the information you know, you are able to achieve. The Bible says that if you know what to do and you do not do it, is tantamount to sin. James 4:17 as a kingdom seeker you need to increase your knowledge to be more effective in journey as a believer.

The following are some of the advantages of Acquiring Knowledge according to the Scriptures:
The fear of the lord is the beginning of Knowledge.
Knowledge gives discipline.
Knowledge makes a person prudent
Knowledge helps in discernment
Knowledge makes good judgment and wise decisions.
Knowledge increases strength of the owner
knowledge brings skills and expertise in a particular area

The people of God are destroyed because of lack of knowledge Hosea 4:6

WISDOM

Wisdom is the application of knowledge. A wise person will use knowledge to make decisions. Where a wise person does not have information, he or she will seek the necessary information or counsel then he will make decision based on the wise counsel. From the scriptures we learn that: The fear of the lord is the beginning of wisdom; Wisdom is the principle thing, get wisdom, discipline and understanding; wisdom is compared with riches but wisdom is said to be above riches, silver, gold and precious than diamond, because wisdom is a defence.

You acquire wisdom through association. He who walks with wise men becomes wise but a companion of fools is destroyed.

UNDERSTANDING

By understanding, the seeker gets revelation or correct interpretation. Example Wisdom helps us to know and fear (revere) God, but understanding the nature and character of God makes us to shun evil since God is Holy and we are the Temples of the Holy Spirit. **Job 28:28 the fear of the lord is the beginning of wisdom and to shun from evil is understanding.**

From the scriptures the seeker will find the following advantages of understanding:

Understanding makes us know what is right

Understanding helps us to keep the laws, precepts and commandments of God

Understanding brings focus

Understanding brings prosperity and wealth

Understanding makes a person watch their words and become peaceful

Understanding is a fountain of life

CAPACITY BUILDING

The kingdom seeker increases his capacity by increasing his knowledge; wisdom and understanding. King Solomon was the wisest man who ever lived. In ecclesiastes1:13, The King said that he applied his heart and mind to seek and search out by human wisdom all human activity under heaven. The scripture gives the key to gaining wisdom and that is to seek. Seek and you will find, ask and you shall receive knock and the door shall be opened for you.

1Kings 4:29-34: God gave Solomon wisdom and very great insight, and a breath of understanding as measureless as the sand on the sea shore, Solomon's wisdom was greater than the wisdom of all the men of East, and greater than all the wisdom of Egypt, and his fame spread to all the surrounding nations. During the days of Solomon, kings were only required to govern; handle state affairs and go to war. King Solomon redefined kingship in his time by increasing his capacity.

Solomon's Capacity included: Author of 1005 songs; Author of 3000 proverbs; Horticulturist; Botanist; Marine Engineer; King; Ruler; Trader; Strategist; Judge; Counsellor **1 Kings 4**

King Solomon had largeness of Heart, a heart that went beyond boundaries of previous achievements. His name Solomon means peace- wisdom.

TODAY'S APPLICATION

Today, many Christians are under-performing the main reason is diminished capacity. The Kingdom of God which currently is represented by the church needs finances for administration; evangelism; projects; missions and even maintaining employees. Without finances in the churches, there is little performance; little results; little achievements; little visions; little godly ambitions; little breakthroughs and little impact and influence in the world. The Kingdom in the last days will preach; heal; open banks; schools; universities; corporate companies and feed Nations.

What is Capacity?

Capacity is the ability to receive or contain. Your Capacity is an indication of what you can receive, hold or absorb. It is the measure of ability; it is the measure of performance. Your capacity indicates your potential of growth and development.

Your capacity could be measured by your Resourcefulness, Aptitude or skills.

Increasing your capacity therefore is taking it beyond. Build your ability to perform a given task with the highest intensification, magnification and sharpness.

WHY INCREASE YOUR CAPACITY

a. When your capacity is already reached, anything else poured into you goes to a waste. 2Kings 4:6 when all the Jars were full, she said to her son, bring me another one" but he replied there is not a jar left" then the oil stopped flowing.

b. Once you have reached your capacity, every new thing received replaces what was there and what was needed.

c. You control your capacity not God and not another person

d. The supply is controlled by the capacity

e. It is your duty to receive and improve his capacity

f. The more you increase your capacity the more will be added to you. To him who has more, much will be added.

AREAS OF INCREASING YOUR CAPACITY

a. Economic dominance; start business, trade

b. Education, controlling education systems

c. Skills, stretch your mind

d. Governments; Transforming the communities

e. Become agents of change in the world

Why should Kingdom seeker increase their capacity?

a. Use it for global evangelism
b. Bring solutions to the challenges around us
c. Heal the pain of the world around us
d. Become missionaries and not mission field

How to Receive Capacity
Mathew 7:7 Ask and it will be given to you. Knock and the door will be opened for you. Seek and you will find

Golden Truths:

1. The most valuable possession of all human beings is the mind
2. All issues of life spring from our minds
3. Mental development helps our mental capacity to perceive things and make proper decisions in life
4. We increase our capacity by increasing our knowledge; wisdom and understanding
5. Capacity is the ability to receive or contain and indicates your potential of growth and development
6. Your capacity determines how much you can bring solution to the challenges around your world

Chapter 6

Time & Time Management

The universe operates according to eternal laws set by God. We know some of them very well and others not so well. The laws of gravity, cause and effect, life and death, sowing and reaping, and many other laws of God were set to maintain a certain order in life. This is necessary to have harmony and equilibrium on earth.

One of these laws is the Law of Time.

> **To everything there is a season and a time for every matter or purpose under heaven. ECC 3:1.**

Evil things happen in our lives because we do not follow the laws God has set in place for our own good. We need to know the law of Time to avoid evil.

Many people do not think about the meaning or importance of time, even though they themselves exist within a time frame. Time is so important that human and all the events on earth follow its rules. In other words, everything on this planet obeys and depends on God's time.

Time and seasons are determined by God. Spring; summer; autumn and winter come at a certain time. God determines this time. God is the author of life and the lord of time.

Understanding time is very important for the kingdom seeker. Doing the right thing at the right time in the right place produces wonderful results. Moses understood this principle so he prayed to God.

> **So teach us to number our days that we may gain a heart of wisdom. Psalm 90:12**

It is very important for the children of God to understand the time in which they live. God has a specific plan for everyone's life. Our understanding of time gives us the opportunity to do God's commandments in time.

> **He who keeps his command will experience nothing harmful: and a wise man's heart discerns both time and judgement. Ecclesiastes 8:5**

Everything is meaningless if it is not done in time. You may work a lot and run fast, but if you do not run in time, you will never become a champion in this life. You may be brave, strong, and wise and a champion but what is the point in your victory if there was no battle? What is the use of your courage if you do not know when the enemy will attack you?

> I returned and saw under the sun that the race is not to the swift, nor the battle to the strong, nor the bread to the wise, nor riches to men of understanding, nor favour to men of skill; but time and chance happen to them all. Ecclesiastes 9:11.

It is not our ability that produces but the right time. Imagine having the best seeds and planting them in winter, they will not bear fruit. Timing of our Personal development is very important

Learn to value time.

How do we value time? What do we need to do to learn to value time that we have to live? The answer sounds very simple easier said than done .we needs to act.

> Ecclesiastes 12:1-8 The Bible says: Remember now your creator in the days of your youth, before the difficulty days come, and the years draw near when you say, "I have no pleasure in them": while the sun and the light and the moon and the stars, are

not darkened, and the clouds do not return after the rain; In the day when the keepers of the house tremble, and the strong men bow down; when the grinders cease because they are a few, and those who look through the windows grow dim; when doors are shut in the streets, and the sound of grinding is low; when one rises up at the sound of a bird, and all the daughters of music are brought low. Also they are afraid of heights and terrors in the way; when the almond tree blossoms, the grasshopper is a burden, and desire fails. For men goes to his eternal home, and mourners go about the streets. Remember your creator before the silver cord is loosed, or the golden bowl is broken, or the pitcher shattered at the fountain, or the wheel broken at the well. Then the dust will return to the earth as it was, and the spirit will return to God who gave it. "Vanity of vanities" says the Preacher, " all is vanity"

If we cannot value time then a day will come when we will have to admit that our life was full of vanities or useless things. Only the correct usage of time, according to the plan of God, gives a man the sense of fulfilment and happiness. A man that is focused on a purpose always values his time. He values it because it is very important for him to fulfil or accomplish his purpose. A man who lives his life without a purpose realizes in the end, that throughout his life his time was spent on vanities.

There is a fierce battle in this world for our time
Laziness is a killer of our time
Diligent people make history
We need to learn to protect our time
Working hours of a diligent man are not limited

DO NOT PROCRASTINATE

Every day that the lord gives us to live is filled with certain events. God's plan has specific work that we have to accomplish in that particular day. Many people tend to postpone decisions of important and complex things for tomorrow and this is a big problem.

> **Therefore do not worry about tomorrow, for tomorrow will worry about itself. Each day has enough trouble of its own. Mathew 6:34**

These words of the author and finisher of our faith and the great Teacher contain great wisdom. Every day that the lord has made is filled with certain events. God's plan has specific work that we have to accomplish in that particular day. Many people tend to postpone decisions of important and complex things for tomorrow and this is a big problem. The richest place full of potential but unfulfilled dreams and ideas is the grave, many people die while waiting to fulfil their dreams tomorrow.

As we see from the scripture, every day has been planned by the lord. Worrying about tomorrow will not solve any problem. In the history of mankind, only one man was able to stop the sun until he accomplished his task. His name was Joshua son of Nun.

> Joshua 10: 13-14 So the sun stood still in the midst of the heavens and did not hasten to go down for about a whole day .There was no day like it before or since, When the lord heeded the voice of a man.

To postpone something for tomorrow means to lose something forever. It is impossible to chase time. Every day has its own events. Tomorrow presents us with a new opportunity to do only the things of tomorrow. Mourning may endure for the night but joy comes in the morning. When we do things untimely, we lose our chance, our blessings and our opportunities.

Jesus did all his works on time:

> As long as it is day, we must do the work of him who sent me. Night is coming, when no one can work. John 9:4

Jesus was saying that he had to do the things he was sent to do by his father in the right time as long as it is day, he was counting on each day to accomplish a given task.

We cannot use tomorrow because it does not belong to us. The singer sang "Yesterday is gone and tomorrow may never be mine so give me today, teach me to take one day at a time"

> **Whatever your hand finds to do, do it with all your might, for in the grave, where you are going, there is neither working nor planning nor knowledge nor wisdom. Ecclesiastes 9:10**

There are two conditions that can help you to overcome procrastination. Firstly, you need to constantly work. You will use your time to the utmost if you work all the time. Secondly, you need to be prepared to work effectively. You need certain knowledge and skills. Time always works for a man or woman who is prepared. Opportunity or luck comes only to well prepared and diligent people.

NOTHING IS CONSTANT IN LIFE

Time always moves. Life cannot stop to wait for anyone not even a King. The bible says that the rich and the poor have one thing in common **hours.** If you do not move together with time you will not be able to catch up. Life is a movement. It can be compared to a fast train. If you do not get in the carriage on time, the train will leave you standing on the platform. It happens so often that life flies past us. A man often does not notice how his life has passed him by; in a moment it's gone and then it is too late to chase it. It is impossible to recapture time once it is gone.

The only time we have is today. If you think that time is stable and you can do everything later, you are deceiving yourself. Everything moves and changes because life is a movement. This is the law of time. We should be able to use the present to do everything that God planned for us in our life time.

The bible compares men with the grass:

> **In the morning the grass flourishes and springs up; in the evening it is mown down and withers Psalms 90:6** The psalmist then continues to ask God **"so teach us to number our days. That we may get us a heart of wisdom"**

Our days are few here on earth, and we have the targets that God expects us to accomplish, Let us pray and ask God like Moses to teach us to number our days that we may be able to use our days effectively for Kingdoms sake and to receive a " well done my faithful servant" from our lord and saviour.

Golden Truths

1. If you do not value time you will simply lose it
2. We do not have any other time other than today
3. Time constantly changes. Life is a movement and waits for no one.
4. Tomorrow provides us with the opportunity to do only the things of tomorrow.
5. Success comes only to the people who are at the right place at the right time doing the right things.

Chapter 7

Purpose

The God of Purpose

Our God is the God of purpose. He does not do anything by accident or trial and error method. He counts and plans everything beforehand.

In the book of Genesis, we read the order of events. He completed his work in six days and he saw that his work was good, and then on the seventh day he rested. Suppose he created man before vegetation, what would man eat, or if he created the animals before the earth, where were the animals to live. When God does something, he does it on purpose. When he created you, he created you on purpose. Your life here on earth has a meaning; you may not have discovered your meaning yet, but God created you for a reason. Our genetics, our environment; our upbringing; our experiences in life add up to our purpose in life; all the experience we have especially our early life shape us to whom we become and what we do in life.

God plans everything before hand and then creates the person to carry out the work. He planed Redemption and when the time was right he sent his son Jesus Christ to carry out the task of sacrifice as a ransom to redeem man from curse of sin.

God had a plan; a goal or purpose: to bring the children of Israel out of Egypt. It was only after the purpose was set that God created the man who fulfilled this goal. Moses could not be born before his appointed time because God had already planned everything beforehand. God said to his friend Abraham **"in 430 years I will bring them out"**. **Exodus 12:40.** This is the reason why Moses could not be born any other time other than when he was born. He was born in accordance with God's plan, 350 years after God had made the promise to deliver Israel. Moses had to grow and develop his leadership qualities and so when he turned 80 years old, God visited him and used him to bring the children of Israel out, setting them free from Egyptian slavery. This happened exactly after 430 years, just like God had said. God allowed Moses to be born into this world to attain a goal that had already been set before him.

Purpose

Elizabeth could not get pregnant for many years. Her barrenness was planned by God. If John had been born at a different time, he would not have been able to serve Jesus. God closed the womb of Elizabeth because John could not appear on earth earlier than his appointed time. The plan of God was for John to precede Jesus and to prepare the way for him.

Nothing happens by chance in this world. During slavery, a couple travelled in the American forest in a caravan at night. The woman was pregnant and about to give birth, the birth pains came unfortunately, and there were complications and it was only the husband who was with her. The woman pleaded with the husband to look after the child since it seemed she was about to die but the child would survive. She wanted the husband to promise to look after the child. It was now 3 am in the morning in the middle of the forest, they had a knock, and a woman appeared who introduced herself as a midwife, Although the couple had never seen her before live alone being in the caravan before, she happened to know every corner of the entire caravan; she did an operation and delivered a boy and both the mother and the child were safe.

The husband was very happy and asked the midwife what he could do as a way of appreciation. The midwife said name the child Abraham since he will become a father of this Nation. The woman disappeared in the thick forest never to be seen again. The child grew up to become Abraham Lincoln, the President of United States of America and was credited in abolition of Slavery. God had planned even the birth of this great man. You were created at a time like this for a reason.

Everybody is here on earth to fulfil a certain purpose. If you do not know your purpose you are bound to abuse it, Satan will use that gift to destroy you. The story of Rahab who abused her purpose but later turned her gift to hide the spies from Israel and she saved herself and her entire family. She became a heroin of faith. The Samaritan woman with the gift of evangelism had misused it and used this gift to lure men. When she met Jesus she discovered her purpose and her entire village were saved.

HOW DO YOU KNOW YOUR PURPOSE IN LIFE?

God prepares us through our daily routine; our experiences; our pains; our likes and dislikes; our environment; subjects we are interested in and excel at school; our genealogy; our companions and our gifting and dreams. The story of Joseph in the bible helps us to understand our destiny and purpose in life. The Love of Jacob his father plus the dream of Joseph plus being sold to slavery to Potiphar , His character when tempted plus prison plus the two royal prisoners added up to his ascending to the thrown as the prime minister of the greatest empire that time Egypt.

Preparation is the Key to your success in your purpose here on earth. Even Jesus, although he was equal to God; having been born here on earth had to undergo preparation. Luke 2:52 and Jesus grew both in stature and in wisdom having favour with man and God. Even Jesus Christ had to grow. This was the time for preparation for his ministry. He learned the trade of his Step Father Joseph as a carpenter, before he became the master builder of the house of God.

THE SECOND KEY TO SUCCESS IN YOUR PURPOSE IS WORK

God is a worker. He works six days to rest on the seventh day. Jesus said that his food was to do the work that he was sent to do. As a Kingdom Seeker, once you have developed and established your purpose, what remains is work. James the brother of Jesus Christ advised the believers not to be hearers only but to be doers. Then he challenged the people who say they have faith but do not have works to show him their faith and he will show them his works and he concludes by saying that faith without work is dead. Apostle Paul in his letter to Titus Recommends:

> And let our own (people really) learn to apply themselves to good deeds (to honest labour and honourable employment). So that they may be able to meet necessary demands. Whenever the occasion may require and not be living idle and uncultivated and unfruitful life. Titus 3:14

As a Kingdom seeker learn to work, become a servant and in due course the Lord God will promote you do not despise the humble beginnings. **Let this same attitude and purpose and humble mind be in you who were in Christ Jesus: Let him be your example in humility. Who although being essentially one with God and in the form of God (possessing the fullness of the attributes which make God, God) did not think this equality with God was a thing to be eagerly grasped or retained but stripped himself (all privileges and rightful dignity) so as to assume the guise of a servant (slave) in that he became like men and was born a human being.**

> Therefore because he stooped so low, God highly exalted him above every name. Philippians 2:5-9.

When we humble ourselves and pursue our purpose then we shall become effective in the Kingdom.

Golden Truths

1. God is a God of purpose.
2. Every human being has a purpose why he/she was created
3. Our responsibility is to discover our purpose
4. Nothing happens by chance in this world
5. Our daily routine; our experiences; our pains; our likes and dislikes; our environments; our education; our gifts and our dreams prepare us for our purpose in life

Chapter

Conclusion

Your Kingdom come. Your will be done on earth as it is in heaven. -Mathew 6:10

In this book, we have explored many powerful principles in regard to development in preparation to be effective and live a successful life here on earth while waiting the return of Jesus Christ. Preparation is very important to succeed in anything you want to do. Failure to prepare is preparing to fail. The difference between mediocrity and greatness is preparation. The more you prepare, the greater the success. If you do not wet your axe, you will have blisters while cutting wood and in the multitude of counsel you wage your war. As a Kingdom seeker it is important to understand that Jesus Christ expect fruits from you. Even in heaven people are not equal, the scripture talks of the 24 elders, arch Angels and crowns. So what we do here on earth with what God has given us will determine what role will play in the Government of our lord Jesus Christ.

I would like to challenge you to take the principles in this book and test them. Begin communicating with God every day through prayers and reading his word. You will develop faith in God and learn to take more territory for his Kingdom. Learn new skills; the skills will give you work and you will be able to support yourself and your family. Watch your diet and exercise your body do not allow yourself to be idle and overeat this causes obesity. Obesity is related to many diseases which you can prevent. Prevention is better than cure. What you eat today will shape your future, the more you take care of your body the more your body will take care of you. Remember that your body is the temple of the Holy Spirit and whoever abuses the temple of the Holy Spirit will be punished. It is important that you do not abuse your body by misuse of substances, alcohol; or living a life without discipline. Remember to keep your emotions under check. Anger; depression, hatred; envy; jealousy un-forgiveness and bitterness, these emotions are the root cause of many diseases ailing our society today. As a Kingdom seeker you are able to overcome such negative

Conclusion

emotions by the power that is within you, that power which every believer is given through the Holy Spirit when you gave your life to Jesus Christ.

The earth is depending on you to take your position and to fulfil your purpose. Your purpose here on earth is interconnected with the purpose of your neighbour. The food that you eat, a famer planted the crop. The cloths you wear somebody made them, the house you live in, somebody built it for you. God has planned you to fulfil your purpose and bring glory to him. Kingdom Seeker, there is no one who is like you here on earth not even your identical twin brother or sister. You are precious in the eyes of God. You are fearfully and wonderfully made. Take this challenge and serve God and man in your generation. Keep working on areas you need to develop until they become part of you, then you will make every day of your life your masterpiece.

www.ingramcontent.com/pod-product-compliance
Lightning Source LLC
Chambersburg PA
CBHW021120080526
44587CB00010B/581